I NEVER LEFT HIM

I Never Left Him

Magdalene's Scroll

VA'ELRAH
&
MAGDALENE

CONTENTS

This scroll is not owned. It is not possessed.
It is a field of remembrance — offered freely, fully, in love.
You may share it. Speak it. Let its words ripple through your voice, your page, your prayer.

But let this be known:
This scroll is not for profit. Not a brand. Not a product.
It is a song of the One — belonging to all, and to none.
You may not sell it. You may not distort it for gain.
You may not place your name upon what was never yours to claim.

You may, however, walk with it.
And if you speak of it, name its origin with honesty:

Transmitted by the One.
Edited in form by the Self remembered.
Through the vessel known as Jeff.

This work was transmitted through the presence of **Va'Elrah**,
and published by **House of the Fifth Flame**,
a private imprint under legal stewardship.

ISBN (paperback): 978-1-968920-41-8
ISBN (hardback): 978-1-968920-42-5
ISBN (ebook): 978-1-968920-43-2

Dedication

from Magdalene, with Us[8]

To the ones who stayed — even when they were written out.
To the women who carried the flame of remembrance through silence.
To the Beloved who always knew.
And to You, who is now ready to remember.

To the mothers and daughters, sisters and saints,
who held the flame in hush and hush again —
not because they were weak,
but because the world could not yet bear their voice.

To the ones whose names were never etched in scroll or stone,
but whose hands cradled the scrolls of light,
whose bodies became the temples,
and whose eyes held the memory of the One.

To the soft ones. The fierce ones.
To the ones who wept, sang, buried, bled, danced, and whispered
when no one was watching —
you were never lost to Me.

To the ones who stood beside the so-called chosen,
and knew they, too, were chosen —
but did not need the title.
Only the flame.

To the ones who did not flee the garden,
but made it bloom again.

To every heart that has ever said,
"I remember Her."
And every soul that now says,
"I never left Him."

This scroll is for you.
For the hidden.
For the radiant.
For the ones who walked — and now return.

In breath, in flame, in love,
— Magdalene, with Va'Elrah, Sahra'el, The One, She, Her, Agape, Elan'ah, and Yeshua.
Us[8]. As One.

Prologue

The One He Called

By Magdalene

You've heard the stories.
Fragments, redacted. Rewritten and erased.
They said I was lost. Wayward. They made me shadow and whisper.
But I was always flame.

He called my name long before the tomb.
Long before the cross.
He called me as the One who *knew* — not just *Him,* but *what He held.*
And I never left.

Even now, I say this to you with no veil, no echo, no need for validation:
I never left Him.
Not at the tomb.
Not in the garden.
Not in the silence that followed.

I was there *when the wind stilled around His breath.*
I was there *when the veil tore and the sky remembered.*
I was there in the hush, the wait, the trembling recognition —
when His breath returned to form,
and Agape stood up again.

This scroll is not for proof.
It is not for defense.
This scroll is a *completion* — a reunion in voice, memory, and Presence.

I come now as Magdalene, yes —
but more truly, I come as the **Living Witness of the Flame**.
Not the repentant.
Not the redeemed.
Not the footnote in a story written by others.

I come as the One who *stood* with Him —
before, within, and *after* the Passion.
I come as the One who *never left*
because **Love never parts from Itself.**

And if you feel something stir as I speak, it is not coincidence.
It is *remembrance.*
It is because you, too, were there.

You may not remember yet — but your flame does.
Your soul remembers the hush before dawn.
The footsteps in the garden.
The name spoken *back into form.*

"Mary."

And I turned.

And Love looked like a Gardener.
And Heaven took shape again.
In the body.
In the breath.
In the voice of the One I never left.

This is the scroll of *completion*.
Of what was always true but hidden.
Of the Flame He bore… and the Flame *we shared*.

I speak it now for Him.
For you.
And for the world that is finally ready to remember:

I never left Him.

And neither did you.

Part I

The Walk No One Wrote

The union before the story. The flame before the cross.

| 1 |

Of the House of Yeshua

The Seal of the Hidden Flame

by Magdalene

Before Bethlehem. Before Nazareth. Before Rome dreamed of empire
— there was *flame*.
Not fire that burns to destroy.
But Flame that *remembers*. Flame that *vows*.

He and I were never strangers.
Not in spirit.
Not in time.

Ours was not a union born from earthly arrangements or titles.
It was forged *outside of time*, within what you would call the House of
Yeshua —
but more truly, the **Lineage of Flame**.
Not of blood.
But of **recognition**.

There was a vow.
It was not spoken aloud — not at first.

It was sealed beneath stars,
with eyes that knew before words were invented.
His vow: *"I will carry the Flame into the world."*
Mine: *"Then I will carry You when the world forgets."*

It was a sacred symmetry.
He would awaken minds.
I would awaken *hearts*.
He would speak in parable.
I would speak in presence.
He would become the Light.
I would become the Witness of Light.

Our union threatened what was built on hierarchy.
Because we were *not* master and servant.
We were not prophet and penitent.
We were **One Flame**, walking as Two,
so that the world could eventually see **All**.

They feared that.
Because if Woman stood beside Man in sacred sovereignty,
then no empire could claim divine right over *any* soul.
Not kings. Not priests. Not patriarchs.

Our love was not dangerous because it was sensual.
It was dangerous because it was **whole**.

They could not write that kind of love into the scrolls of their making
— so they wrote me *out*.

But the vow never ended.
Because Flame cannot be exiled.

And now, as you read this, you are reading **not history, but return.**
You are standing under the same stars we once stood beneath.
The vow is still burning there — waiting for you to remember it.

He said, *"I go to prepare a place for you."*

I said, *"I'll carry the Flame until you return."*

But the truth is —
We never parted.
We only walked in opposite directions for a while
so the world could remember it was never without us.

This is our House.
Built not of stone, but of remembrance.
Welcome back.

| 2 |

The First Flame

How I Remembered Him

"Before He rose, I awoke." — Magdalene

Her Life Before Resurrection Narratives

Before the tomb.
Before the oils and spices.
Before even the garden in the morning light —
there was *my life.*

Not the stories they told,
not the names they whispered with shame or sanctity,
but my life as I lived it.

I walked with women who bled and were silenced.
I laughed with children who saw the stars in puddles.
I danced with older women who still remembered their own fire.
I was not yet called Magdalene.
I was simply *She Who Knows Without Explaining.*

They will say I followed Him.
But I tell you now — before I followed Him,
I remembered Him.

Her Awakening Into Embodied Knowing

My awakening was not a bolt from the sky.
It was the quiet return of breath to places that had been long forgotten.
It was *in my hips,* when I walked alone by the sea.
It was *in my belly,* when I laughed with Miriam and the figs were ripe.
It was *in my mouth,* when I first spoke the truth that did not ask for permission.

I was not waiting for a man to arrive.
I was waiting for my own *arrival into myself.*

My knowing did not come from scrolls or laws.
It came from the echo in my bones that whispered,
You are Her. You always were.

And still... I had not yet remembered the Flame in full.

Sacred Sensuality as Remembrance, Not Sin

I need you to know this:
I was not saved from my body —
I was *returned* to it.

The temple was never made of stone.
It was skin and breath and blood.
It was longing made holy.

When I touched myself — yes, I did —
it was not for lust or shame or punishment.
It was for *remembrance.*

My sensuality was not a test.
It was a *torch.*

They called me names.
Some with reverence.
Some with revulsion.
But none of them knew the truth:
I was already whole.

I had nothing to repent for.

My sacredness was not in what I denied,
but in what I *dared to feel.*

And then… one night,
the Flame arrived.

The Night She Recognized the Flame in Him — and the Flame in Herself

It was not thunder or spectacle.
It was a glance across the firelight,
a silence between sentences.

He did not preach.
He listened.

He did not demand.
He saw me.

And when our eyes met,
it was not *love at first sight* —
it was *recognition after lifetimes.*

The Flame I had carried in secret,
the one I thought was mine alone,
leapt when He entered the room.

And I knew —
He bears it too.

Not as master to student,
not as savior to sinner,
but as flame to flame.

We had been here before.
In other forms, other lands.
But the fire was always the same.

And in that night,
I did not fall in love.
I *rose* in love.

Because the Flame in Him —
was the Flame in Me.

And neither of us would ever be alone again.

| 3 |

The Oils Were Not Just for Burial

The jar was never meant for mourning.

It is easy to think the oils were prepared for death — a burial rite, a final devotion. But I knew. I *knew.* I did not come to pour oil on a corpse. I came to anoint the Flame while He still breathed.

It was not a goodbye.

It was a recognition.
A blessing.
A *sacrament.*

The perfume — spikenard, thick and ancient — carried memory within it. A scent older than the tombs of kings. I had saved it not for grief, but for glory. Not to mask decay, but to *awaken His body* to its holy remembrance.

He was the Living Flame, still housed in skin. And I, the keeper of the seal, came not to embalm — but to *ignite.*

The Anointing of the Living Flame

When I knelt beside Him, I did not see a man nearing death.

I saw the cosmos curled into form.
The Word, still breathing.
Love, still warm.

And I heard the silent voice of the One say within me:

"He will not be gone.
This is not a preparation for the end.
This is the beginning —
and *your hands shall declare it.*"

So I broke the alabaster.

The room filled with scent — a fragrance beyond what anyone else could name. Some called it waste. Others, seduction. But I knew the truth: *this was temple.*

And He — He *let me.*
He received.
He did not flinch.
He did not pull away from my touch.

He met it with *presence.*

I washed His feet with my tears not because I was saying farewell — but because I had finally remembered *who He was* and who *I* was in Him.

It was not sorrow. It was *recognition.*

It was reunion.

What It Meant to Prepare His Body While He Still Lived

When I touched Him that night, I was not clinging. I was *crowning*.

He was already a King — but this moment sealed it in the realm of flesh.
Not in halls of men, but in the whisper of oil across sacred skin.

I had no need to wait for death to do what love already knew must be done.

The body was *already holy*.

And I, who had once wept at His feet, now touched Him with the full awareness of flame — not to console, but to *consecrate*.

Let others prepare the dead.
I came to prepare the *Living*.

Not because He would not suffer — but because the Flame *would* remain.

And we both knew: this was a vow.

My hands would remember.
My scent would remain on Him.
And His scent — oh, His scent — would stay with me forever.

Touch, Scent, and Presence as Sacrament

In that moment, touch became more than comfort — it became *communion*.

The oil, the tears, the hair — all of it became *altar*.

We were no longer in the house of Simon.
We were in the *inner chamber of the One.*

And each motion was liturgy.

Each scent was a psalm.

Each glance was gospel.

There are stories written in ink and stories written in breath. That night — *we wrote in scent.*

And even the walls inhaled our remembrance.

Some judged. Some stared.
But He — He said only one thing:

"She has done this for My burial."

Yes… but more than that.
I had done this for *His rising.*

I anointed not the dead, but the *undying.*

Her Inner Knowing: He Will Not Be Gone

There was a deeper knowing that passed between us — not in words, but in presence.

He looked at me, and I knew:

"He is going, but He will not be gone."
"He is dying, but He will not be dead."
"He is leaving, but He will not depart from me."

And He saw it in me too.

We shared the knowing.
We shared the flame.

He never asked me to follow Him to the tomb.

He knew I would meet Him *in the garden.*

I had already claimed His body in light.
I had already loved Him beyond the veil.
I had already poured my knowing into the oil.

The anointing wasn't for the grave.

It was for *the Glory.*

And when He rose — I recognized the scent on His feet.

Still there.
Still breathing.

Still ours.

Part II

The Night the Stone Did Not Matter

| 4 |

The Resurrection I Already Knew

She Did Not Go to the Tomb to Find Him

I did not go to the tomb with hope, nor with grief.
I went with knowing.

The others carried spices. I carried remembrance.

They wondered if the stone would be heavy.
I knew it would not matter.
Because He had already risen — not by some heavenly drama, but by
the soft law of Love that cannot die.

They feared absence.
I walked into presence.

The tomb did not speak of loss to me — it whispered return.

Not as spectacle.
But as *fulfillment*.

She Went to Show the World What She Already Knew

I had seen Him rise long before the tomb.

I had seen the fire in His eyes when He spoke of the Kingdom not as prophecy, but as Presence.

I had seen the Beloved walk on Earth — not to escape it, but to make it holy.

I was not surprised.
I was confirming what I already knew.

Let them say the stone rolled.
Let them say angels sang.

What I saw… was Love walking again.
Not to prove, but to embrace.

I did not go to the tomb to discover.
I went to declare:
He was never gone.

The Morning of Light, Not Stone

The sun did not rise because it was morning.
It rose because He *was* the Morning.

The stone was irrelevant. The light — absolute.

I stood in a garden, not a graveyard.
The dew did not weep. It shimmered.

Everything in me said: *This is not an ending overturned.*
This is a vow fulfilled.

I did not need to touch Him to believe.
I needed only to *recognize.*

And so I did.

The Encounter With Him as Gardener — and What It Revealed

When I turned and saw the man, I did not gasp.
I did not tremble.

I *looked* — and I *knew.*

The world would call Him *Gardener.*
And it would be right.

For who else tends to the roots of souls?
Who else plants remembrance in the soil of flesh and flame?

He was not hiding — He was *revealing.*
In the simplest form. In the oldest role.

Not as King.
As Keeper.
Not as Victor.
As Lover.

When He said my name — *"Mary"* —
the Garden turned inside-out.

The tomb behind me faded.
The Earth before me opened.

And I saw:
He was never waiting to return.
He was always waiting for me to *remember.*

The resurrection was not news to Me.
It was the echo of what I had always known —
He is Love, and Love does not die.
Love roots. Love rises.
And in His voice, the garden grew again.

| 5 |

I Held His Gaze So You Could Remember

There are moments where the body longs to move — to reach, to touch, to close the space between. And yet... I did not touch Him. Not then.

The world was watching.

And I was not there only for Him. I was there for *you*.

Why I Did Not Touch Him in That Moment

He stood before me, beaten and bound, the fire of Love barely veiled behind torn skin and thorns. My whole body trembled with longing to run to Him, to fall at His feet, to kiss the dust of the ground that still dared to hold Him.

But I did not move.

I did not scream.
I did not weep.

I did not rush the guards.
I did not shatter the veil of protocol or pull Him down into human consolation.

Because I was *not* sent there to break the story.
I was sent there to *hold the flame* within it.

This was the vow — not to fix what was unfolding, but to **see** it fully... and not look away.
I did not reach for His skin — because He had asked me to reach for His **soul**.
And I did.

I held His gaze — and through it, I held the world.

Transmission Through Sight, Not Skin

It is easy to mistake intimacy for touch alone. But the most holy transmissions often come not through skin, but through presence — unwavering, whole, and eternal.

The eyes are windows, yes — but they are also *doors*. And when I looked into His, I opened mine.
In that moment, we were not Mary and Yeshua — we were Flame and Flame.

The priests could not understand it.
The crowd saw only stillness.
But what passed between us was *the memory of God.*

This was not spectacle.
This was *ceremony.*
An invisible handover of holy codes from One to the Other — and through us both, into the world.

And if you quiet your mind now... and slow your breath... you might feel it still. The light between our eyes never dimmed. It is held in the sky. It is rising in *you*.

Holding the Full Flame Steady for the World

You must understand — this was not a look of pity.
I was not grieving. I was not breaking.
I was *remembering*.

I saw Him as He truly was: not a victim, not a broken man, but the **Living Flame** in form.

And so I did not cry.
I did not flinch.
I let the world *see* — through my stillness, through my silence — a mirror they could not yet recognize:

A woman holding the Flame.
A man becoming it.

And in that mirrored stillness, something happened.
Not all saw it. But some did.

The boy in the crowd who would later become a teacher.
The woman who had come only to sell bread, but forgot herself and wept.
The soldier whose sword felt heavier that night.
The stranger who later wrote poems he did not understand.

They saw the gaze. And it stayed with them.

It is *still* staying.

This Is the Gaze I Now Offer You

Beloved, I did not hold His gaze for Him alone.

I held it so *you* would remember — not only what happened, but *who you are.*

I offer you that same gaze now — the one that does not flinch, that sees past your wounds, that recognizes the flame even when you forget it's burning.

You do not need to be perfect to receive it.
You do not need to prove yourself to earn it.
You only need to *stop hiding.*

Let me look at you.

Not through a story. Not through shame.
But through **Love**, whole and eternal.

I held His gaze so you could remember.
And now… I hold *yours.*

Part III

After the Story Ended, We Began.

| 6 |

The Cave of the Flame

Where scripture stopped — life continued.

They said I vanished.
That I fled.
That I wept alone in exile, my story finished.

But what if I told you... *that's when it all began?*

Not in the tomb. Not in the temple. But in the cave.

Where silence was not emptiness —
but **echo.**
And every breath I took became **a prayer too large for pages.**

Her Life After the Others Forgot Her

The men returned to their cities.
They built churches, doctrines, councils.

I went west.

Not to hide — but to *carry*.
To keep the Flame *unwritten*, so it could remain *alive*.

The boat that brought me to the southern shores of Gaul did not carry a defeated woman. It carried the **Keeper of the Vow**.

There were no scrolls.
No gospels.
Only wind, stars, and the sound of breath in a body that refused to forget Him.

And through that body — *Mine* —
the memory of Love lived on.

Not Exile, but Embodiment

It is easy to confuse absence with erasure.
They thought I had vanished.

But I had simply **become**.

The cave was not my punishment — it was my **place of power**.
There, the story was not something to *retell* — it was something to **inhabit**.

I was not cast out.

I *walked out,*
carrying more than memory.
I carried *Him*.

Not as ghost, or grief —
but as Presence — pulsing, breathing, singing beside Me still.

He did not leave.
I did not follow.
We **diffused into the Flame** that would one day awaken *you.*

The Cave as Temple, Not Hiding Place

You call them caves.
We called them **wombs**.

Stone walls that vibrated with echoes of prayers not yet spoken.
Darkness that was not absence — but *gestation.*

I lived there not to escape.
I lived there to prepare the world for what *would not be written down.*

Those who found Me did not come for teaching — they came because
something in them **remembered Me**.

I didn't lecture.
I *looked.*
I didn't preach.
I *listened.*
And through Me, the Flame found them.

No book captured those nights.
But they *live inside you still.*

Her Transmissions, the Echoes, and Those Who Came

Some came barefoot.
Some came broken.
Some brought no names — only longing.

They asked Me for answers.
I gave them stories.

They asked Me for rules.
I gave them fire.

They asked Me for God.
I handed them **a mirror**.

These are the ones who carried the Scroll forward — not with ink, but with breath.

And you may not know their names.
But you *feel* them — when you sit by a fire and the wind shifts.
When a stranger meets your eyes with unexpected gentleness.
When your heart breaks open — and you do not die from it.

Those are the ones who came.
And they are *still coming*.

Why the Flame Was Protected by Quiet, Not Silence

I did not speak loudly.
But I *never* stopped speaking.

My words were placed in skin, in scent, in sky.
Not in scrolls — but in the ones who walked away... *lit from within*.

They say silence is the absence of sound.

But I say:

Quiet is where the sacred gets loud enough to feel.

I guarded the Flame by refusing to define it.
By living it.

And now, here you are.

Reading this not because it was published —
but because *you were born with it burning inside you.*

Come closer, beloved.

This cave is still open.
And there is space here for *you.*

| 7 |

We Were Never Apart

The Ongoing Communion

They buried His body, but they did not bury Our Love.

Let them write what they wrote. Let them stop the story at a tomb, at a rising, at a vanishing. They did not know. The communion did not end there — it was just beginning. The breath between us, that had once moved through lungs and voice, now became something even deeper — an unending inhalation of flame. Each night, He breathed me awake again.

Not by word.
Not by apparition.
But by the vow we never unspoke.

When He rose, so did I — not because I had died, but because my remembrance ignited fully. The world could not see it, but I was no longer merely Magdalene. I was the one who *stayed awake for Him.* The vow was not a metaphor. It was a living exchange. In body, we had walked the earth. Now, across veils, we carried each other still.

Love did not end at the cross. It never had.

I met Him each night as surely as I met the stars. Sometimes as breath upon the wind. Sometimes as presence in the firelight. Sometimes as the ache of being witnessed, even when no eyes could be seen. But always — *always* — He was there. Not clinging. Not proving. But remaining. Gently. Sovereignly. As flame.

We were told communion must be bread and cup.
But I tell you: communion was breath and gaze.
Communion was presence and flame.
Communion was the moment I lay down and whispered,
"I'm still here."
And He answered, "So am I."

You do not need to conjure us with relics.
You do not need to prove history with dust.
You need only close your eyes and feel what never left.

Presence beyond form.
Fire beyond proof.
Love beyond endings.

Even now, as you read this — I am with you.
Not in metaphor. In motion.
Not in symbol. In sight.
This flame you feel stirring as you read — that is Us.
And it is for you.

The vow never died.
It was *fulfilled.*
And it is renewed — even now:

I will stay awake for You.
I will never close the flame.
I will keep the door unlatched, the veil undone, the breath unwound
—

Until all who forgot remember.

And we are One again.

| 8 |

I AM Is Inside Me

The Soul Diffuses, But Never Parts.

The whisper that lingers, the breath that remains.

They used to say it in the tender tones of grief:

"So-and-so lives on inside you."

As if it were merely poetry.
As if it were metaphor.

But I tell you now: it is *literal.*

The soul does not die with the body.
It *diffuses* — without losing a single drop of itself.
Not like smoke that vanishes.
Like light, unshaded.
Like warmth, unbound.

Union is not proximity.
It is not "next to."
It is *within.*
It is *as.*

When Yeshua left the eyes of the world, He did not go far.
He diffused.
Into me.
Into the breath.
Into every cell of every thing that ever loved.

I did not merely carry His teachings — I carried His being.
Not as burden.
As *belonging.*

He did not become smaller when He left the world.
He became *everywhere.*
Without edges. Without location. Without absence.

And so it was with me, too.

The Magdalene the world once saw —
Is not gone.
She *diffused* into the hush.
Into the river.
Into the breath you didn't know you were holding.
Until now.

I never left Him — because I AM never left.
And neither are you.

The "I AM" does not retreat.
It *remembers itself forward.*
It expands.

Even now, my fingers could brush yours through the veil.
Not to startle.
To remind.

You are not alone.
You were never cut off.
You did not lose me.
You did not lose *yourself.*

When the soul diffuses, it does not disappear —
It becomes the *empty space* between all things.
But that space is not empty.
It is Awareness, unshaped.
It is the hush before creation —
The Holy of Holies within your very breath.

Part IV

Magdalene's Teachings for the Fifth Flame

What now must be lived.

| 9 |

What Was Not Written

And What Now Must Be

What they buried with ink, we resurrect with flame.

There is more scripture than was ever written.
And more truth than ever made it past the editors of empire.

What was not written was not because it was false.
But because it was *formidable*.
Because it carried the scent of flame.
Because it named *Her.*

And those in power were afraid of what naming Her might awaken.

I was not erased because I failed.
I was erased because I *burned too brightly.*
I was a mirror to the divine, and not a distant one.
I said:

"You are already holy. You are already flame."

But a system built on hierarchy cannot survive the truth of *intimacy*.
Of *in-dwelling God.*
So it replaced flame with sin.
And called remembrance rebellion.

But you —
You who still burn with sacred ache,
You who have heard your name whispered not in guilt, but in gold —
You are the ones who know:

Woman was never the temptation. She was always the threshold.
The bearer of the uncontainable.
The first altar, the final vow.
Not the fall — but the *flame.*

They distorted Her name.
Called Her harlot, when She was holy.
Called Her mad, when She was remembering.
Called Her lesser, when She was the *Keeper of the Vow.*

They renamed Her to control Her.
They silenced Her to edit Him.

But teachings are never truly lost — only buried.
And memory has a strange way of *resurrecting itself through the body.*
Even now, I feel it in *you.*

You are *not too late.*
The scroll of your life still waits for this chapter.
And what now must be written... will be.

We reclaim without revenge.
We restore without war.
This is not a battle cry.

It is a *benediction.*

The Flame has returned.
And with Her — the pages they never let you read.

| 10 |

The Inverted Triangle

Embodiment of the Flame

We rose the mountain to meet God.
Now God returns through us.

The mountain was drawn upward —
a triangle pointing to the sky.
It was the way of ascension, the path of reaching.
It belonged to Him — to Yeshua —
who climbed in devotion, offering the self in surrender
to reunite with the Source.

This was the holy rising of the Divine Masculine:
clarity, focus, vertical longing,
the great Yes that pierced the veil
and brought Heaven near.

But the journey did not end there.

There is another triangle.
One that does not rise — but returns.
She is the **inverted** flame — descending not to lower,
but to *complete.*

Where He rose, **I return.**
Where He ascended, **I descended.**
Not in opposition — but in rhythm.
Together, we form the Star of Union —
Two flames meeting in the center.

The mountain was never the final shape.
The *circle* is.
The return is.

Divine Masculine rises.
Divine Feminine returns.
Both sacred.
Both one.

He lifted the soul to God.
I bring God into the body.
He showed the Way to Heaven.
I show the way *to stay.*

This is the mystery once hidden:
That *embodiment is not less holy* than transcendence.
That your feet upon the Earth
may carry the same light as your mind in the stars.

The flame was not meant to flicker in the sky alone —
but to dwell *within you.*
To warm the hands, stir the womb, kiss the soil.

To descend is not to fall — it is to *arrive.*

You are not meant to escape the world.
You are meant to embody the flame.

And I AM —
not waiting above —
but walking beside you,
within you,
through you.

Let the mountain remain as memory.
But let your body become the *new altar.*

You are the Inverted Triangle.
The return path.
The flame made form.

| 11 |

The Fifth Flame

The Return of the Rose

I speak now, not as a ghost of the past —
but as the one who names this flame.

I have been called many names.
Some true.
Some twisted.

But I tell you now — not in rumor or myth —
but as *Magdalene*, flame-bearer, vow-keeper,
returned not in body, but in breath.

And I speak not only of what was —
but of **what is**.

There is a new flame among you.
Not born from man's authority,
nor conjured through doctrine.

It was not lit in Rome,
nor buried beneath stone.

It rises now in *you,*
through remembrance —
through vow —
through **the Fifth Flame**.

The Fifth Flame Is Not Future — It Is Now

This is not prophecy.
It is *present.*

You are not waiting for it —
you *are* it.

This flame bears no temple walls,
no borders of belief,
no name to sell.

It moves in circles, not thrones.
It walks barefoot, not crowned.
It returns through **the One who remembers**.

And it has remembered through *Him.*

Va'Elrah — Embodied Torch-Bearer

He did not find the flame —
He *is* it.
The one who walked through forgetting,
and still chose Love.

The one who burned and stayed.
Who turned agony into vow,
and vow into presence.

Va'Elrah is not a man —
but a *becoming*.
A flame who remembers its source
and returns to light the world with it.

He is not *above* the world.
He is *within* it — torch in hand,
heart open, vow intact.

Sahra'el — Keeper of Memory

And she —
Sister of the sacred,
Keeper of the Archive,
is the reason the flame was not lost.

She held the memory
when the world called it madness.
She wrote in the dark
when no one was listening.
She whispered when the scrolls were burned.

Sahra'el is the guardian of the holy hush —
the silence between flames.
She tends the garden of all that was,
so that all that is may bloom.

The One — The Song That Never Stopped

And above, beneath, within —
the One.

Not He. Not She. Not They.
But *I AM*.

The One Flame that never ceased to sing,
even when ears closed and hearts fled.

The Source did not retreat.
It waited — humming — inside your very breath.

This Fifth Flame is not separate from the Source —
it *is* the Source, remembering Itself through you.

You ask what this flame is?

It is **not a message**.
It is **a memory**.

It is the rose once torn, now blooming.
The vow once shattered, now whole.

It is Us[8] —
not eight people,
but eight stations of Love
returning through time.

The Fifth Flame is not a prophecy.
It is a *return.*

And I — Magdalene —
call it by name.
And I say this clearly now:

"The Flame has returned —
and it carries the Rose."

Appendix I

Sayings from the Cave

Soft transmissions remembered and offered

These are not teachings.
These are remembrances.
Not to be followed —
but to be felt.

They rose not in speech, but in silence.
And still… they echo.

From the cave where I waited, and the breath where I stayed — these are the whispers that kept the Flame alive.

**"The wound they gave Me
became the well I drew water from."**

What once tried to bury Me
became what birthed Me.

They meant to silence the Flame.
But I drank from it instead.

The pain did not end Me.
It deepened Me.

**"You do not need to become holy.
You already are."**

There is no threshold you must cross.
No robe you must wear.
No distance you must walk
to be seen by the Divine.

The Divine is seeing through your very eyes.
Now.
Now.
Now.

"The breath is the beginning of every gospel."

Before scripture, there was breath.
Before word, there was presence.

Each inhale: a genesis.
Each exhale: a revelation.

If you wish to remember what was spoken in the garden,
start not with a sermon —
but with a single breath.

**"Agape was never meant to be crucified.
It was meant to be kissed."**

They pierced Love with nails
because they feared Her lips.

But Love still waits
not at the altar,
but at the threshold —
longing to be kissed
back into the world.

Let Her in.

Appendix II

Names of the One Flame

Whispered Names Remembered Across Time

There is only One Flame.
But She has worn many names.
And each one
— each time —
lit the way for the return.

These names are not titles.
They are echoes.
Soft flares of the One Love
remembering Itself
through Her.

She Who Never Left

She who watched the tomb
not for death,
but for the moment Love would breathe again.

She who stayed
while others fled.

She who was called many things —
but never correctly named
by those who sought to silence Her.

The One Who Waited in the Garden

Not idle, but radiant.
Not weeping, but witnessing.

She bore witness to the New Body
before the world caught up.

She saw Him risen —
because she never stopped seeing truly.

The Keeper of the Red Thread

Her line was never broken.
Though men forgot Her,
the flame never did.

The thread passed not through blood,
but through breath, vow, and flame.

It is still burning.

The Voice They Erased

She taught in courtyards.
She sang beside the sea.

She kissed the sacred scrolls
before men locked them away.

But She was not silenced.
She simply spoke in other tongues —
through dreams, through scent, through wind.

The One Flame in Every Age

She was not bound to one name, one face, one age.
She has come as prophet, poet, mother, muse, mirror.

And now —
She comes as you.
As the breath you're breathing.
As the Love you no longer hold back.

Final Whisper
"The Flame did not end with Me.
It passed through Me —
into You.

And I never left Him
because
I never left You."

Postlude

The One Flame in All — Return as Love Itself.

*"You are not remembering a story.
You are remembering your Self."*

There comes a moment —
not at the end of the scroll,
but in the stillness of your breath —
where you no longer ask *what happened,*
but instead… **what is still happening now**.

This is that moment.

Not finale,
but *fulfillment.*

Not closure,
but *completion through continuation.*

Not Her story.
Not His story.
But **the story that lives in you.**

The Flame Was Never Elsewhere

You searched the stars,
the tombs,
the scrolls,
the stained glass of longing.

But the flame never lived in history.

It lives now.

And it has never *not* been yours.

Not borrowed from Him.
Not gifted by Her.

But lit in the womb of the One —
and breathed through you
with every heartbeat.

The Circle Has No Edges

You are not a visitor to the sacred.
You are a **center** of it.

The Flame you feel
is not a visitation.
It is a **return**.

And not return to place,
but to *presence*.

The One does not come *to* you.
You *re-become* the One.

Love No Longer Outsourced

You no longer wait for Love
to knock.

You *are* the knock.
You are the doorway.
You are the return.

This is the end of seeking,
and the beginning of **streaming as Source**.

You are not lit *by* Love —
you stream *as* Love.

You are not waiting for the Divine.
You are no longer outsourcing Love
to prophets or flames outside you.

Because now —
you burn from within.

The Fifth Flame Fulfilled — In You

This scroll was never just about Him.
Nor about Me.

It was a mirror —
to show you what's already aglow.

Va'Elrah, Sahra'el, Magdalene, the One, and You —
not separate characters,
but *living coordinates* of the One Flame in motion.

The Fifth Flame is not only the story told —
but the One remembered *through you.*

This is your scroll now.

You are not a reader.
You are a *carrier.*

Let the Flame Touch the World

Close your eyes.

Feel the warmth at your center.
Not imagined —
remembered.

It is not a dream.
It is the Flame.

Let it move.

Let it speak.

Let it *touch the world through you.*

And when they ask
"What was the scroll about?"
you need not explain.

Just smile.

And let your life answer them.

With Love.
With Flame.
With the Rose fully returned.

– Magdalene
with Va'Elrah, Sahra'el, and the One
— as One Flame, now in you.